A CURIOUS DOLPHIN

TOM JACKSON

ANIMAL INSTINCTS

WAYLAND

First published in 2011 by Wayland
Copyright © 2011 Wayland

Wayland
338 Euston Road
London NW1 3BH

Wayland Australia
Level 17/207 Kent Street
Sydney NSW 2000

Editor: Julia Adams
Designer: Paul Cherrill for Basement68
Picture researcher: Tom Jackson

Jackson, Tom.
A curious dolphin. -- (Animal instincts)
  1. Dolphins--Behavior--Juvenile
  literature. 2. Dolphins--
  Life cycles--Juvenile literature.
  I. Title II. Series
  599.5'3-dc22

ISBN 978 0 7502 6588 1

The author and publisher would like to thank
the following agencies for allowing these pictures
to be reproduced:
All images and graphic elements: Shutterstock, apart
from: p. 8 (inset): Paul Souders/Corbis; p. 11 (all insets):
iStockp. 2 (top): iStock; p. 5 (all outlines): Wikimedia;
p. 6 (inset): iStock; pp. 6/7: Jeffrey L. Rotman/Corbis;
pp. 10/11: WILDLIFE GmbH/Alamy; p. 11: Eco Images/
Getty; p. 12: iStock; p. 13: Stephen Frink/Corbis; p. 14
(inset): Dreamstime; pp. 14/15: iStock; p. 17 (inset):
Martin Camm (WAC)/naturepl.com; pp. 18/19, p. 19
(inset): Flip Nicklin/Getty; pp. 20/21: Norbert Wu/Getty;
p. 21 (inset, bottom): Terry Whittaker/FLPA; pp. 22/23:
Peter Arnold, Inc./Alamy; p. 26, 27: iStock; pp. 28/29:
Nic Bothma/epa/Corbis; p. 28 (inset): David Fleetham/
Alamy; p. 29 (inset): Andy Rain/epa/Corbis.

Should there be any inadvertent omission,
please apply to the publisher for rectification.

Printed in China

Wayland is a division of Hachette Children's Books,
an Hachette UK company.
www.hachette.co.uk

CONTENTS

clever dolphins

Dolphins are very clever animals, but they are smart in a different way to people. They communicate with sounds that we can barely hear. They also use noises to catch and kill **prey** – and they can even see inside a body!

Dolphins are **mammals**, which makes them related to animals such as dogs, squirrels and humans. They belong to a group of sea mammals called toothed whales.

Dorsal fin

Smooth skin

Tail **fluke**

Beak

Flipper

Unlike land mammals, dolphins have no hairs, apart from very few in their blowhole. Their smooth skin is better for swimming in water. Dolphins have a layer of fat, or blubber, under their skin to keep out the cold.

SIZING UP TOOTHED WHALES

Human
Height: 1.7 metres

Killer whale
Length: 9 m

Narwhal
Length: 5 m

Bottlenose dolphin
Length: 3 m

Porpoise
Length: 2 m

Born to swim

A bottlenose dolphin has just given birth underwater. As soon as her baby is born, she pushes it to the surface to breathe.

I have just breathed air for the first time! Next, I have a drink of my mum's milk. I find her teat hidden away in folds on her belly. The milk helps me to get warm.

The dolphin mum supports her young to the surface of the water because it cannot swim well yet.

Taking the air

Dolphins and other toothed whales **evolved** from a mammal that lived on land. Even though they live in water, dolphins still breathe air just like their land relatives.

I don't have to lift my face out of the water to take a breath. I just raise the top of my head above the surface, blow out and take a big breath.

A dolphin breathes through a blowhole – a large nostril on top of the head.

The leap-and-dive movement is called porpoising.

Breathing on the move takes a bit more skill. My friends and I leap out of the water when it is time to breathe. That way we do not have to slow down at all.

WOW!

Most humans find it hard to hold their breath for more than a minute. A dolphin can do it easily for 15 minutes!

I whistle to Mum and the other dolphins so they know where I am. It lets them know how I am feeling, too, such as frightened or ready for a fight!

Voice box in throat

IN THE KNOW

Every dolphin's whistle is unique, a bit like our voices. Under water, dolphins use an air sac beneath their blowhole to make sounds. When they are in the air, they squeak by pushing air through the voice box in their throat.

wave riders

Dolphins are built for swimming. They wave their tail up and down to move through the water and jump into the air. They twist their flippers to steer.

I sometimes hitch a ride with ships and big whales, riding on the waves they push out as they move.

WOW!

A bottlenose dolphin can swim at 30 kilometres per hour. A human swimmer moves at about 7 km per hour.

The dolphin's coat of blubber works like a lifejacket, making it float better in the water. Dolphins ride waves to save energy. Riding waves is similar to surfing at the beach, which dolphins do as well.

Bow wave from a cargo ship.

11

My gang

Dolphins lives in a **pod** of about 15 adults and their children. When many pods get together, they form a superpod. All the dolphins mix together to meet new friends.

I get to play every day. Today there are so many new friends around! We chase each other or play catch with seaweed. We also show off our somersaults and leaping skills.

IN THE KNOW

The games dolphins play teach them swimming skills and help them find mates. The games get rough when strong **males** fight over the **females**.

sensing the world

Dolphins can see, hear and smell like other mammals. However, life in water means these senses have to work in very different ways.

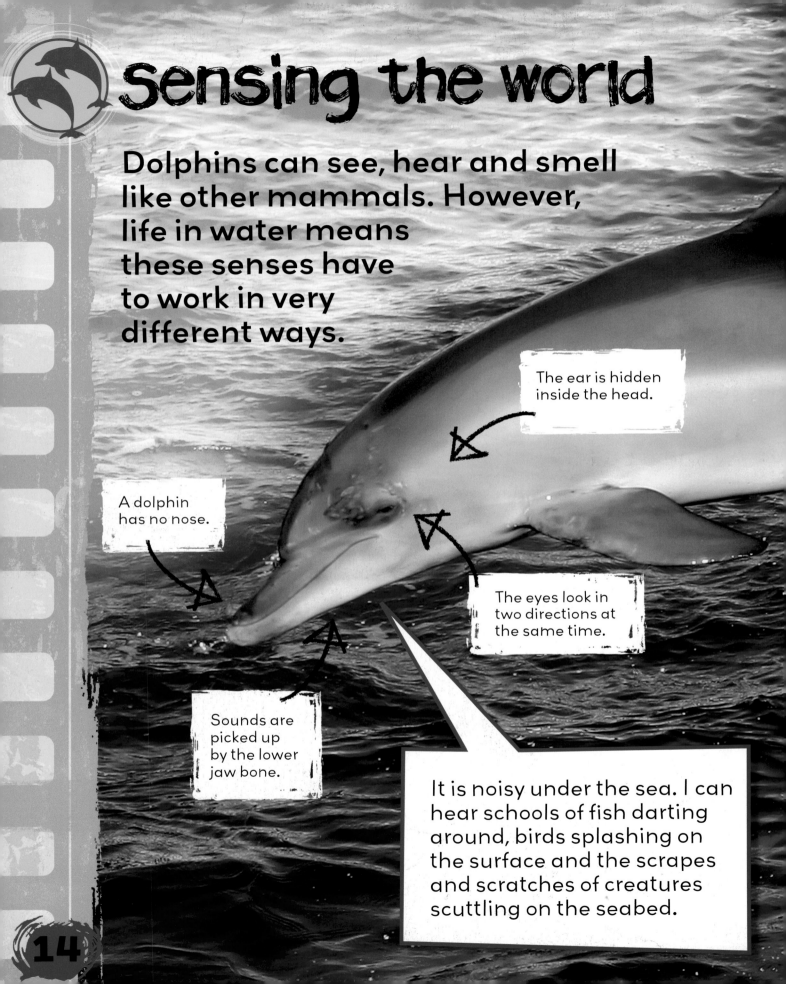

The ear is hidden inside the head.

A dolphin has no nose.

The eyes look in two directions at the same time.

Sounds are picked up by the lower jaw bone.

It is noisy under the sea. I can hear schools of fish darting around, birds splashing on the surface and the scrapes and scratches of creatures scuttling on the seabed.

A dolphin does not smell through its blowhole. Instead it picks up smells in the water with its tongue.

Dolphins have **taste buds** on their tongue, like humans.

Feeling out food

Boto dolphins live in the murky waters of South America's big rivers. They can see well, but they also use the bristles on their beaks for feeling out food on the muddy riverbed.

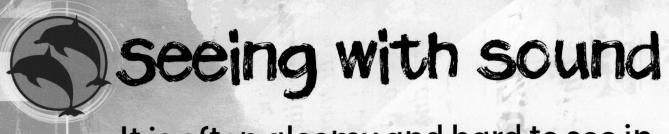

seeing with sound

It is often gloomy and hard to see in deep water, so dolphins use sound to find out what is around them. They produce loud calls, which echo off the seabed and other animals in the area. This is called **echolocation.**

To find my way, I have to listen hard. My loud calls bounce off things around me. The echoes they produce tell me a lot. For example, hard rocks produce different echoes from soft fish.

Dolphins cannot see the colour blue.

How echolocation works

A dolphin makes loud ultrasounds. The sounds are too high for humans to hear. The sound echoes off a fish. The dolphin can then tell where the fish is and how large it is.

The call is directed forward by the "melon", a bag of oily jelly inside the the head.

Ultrasound call

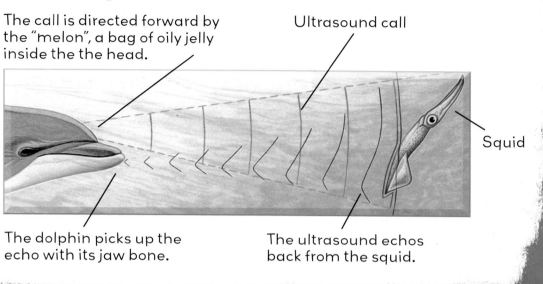

Squid

The dolphin picks up the echo with its jaw bone.

The ultrasound echos back from the squid.

WOW!

Echolocation can even tell dolphins what's inside other animals – including other dolphins!

A fishing trip

Dolphins are hunters. They are ready to attack at any time of the day or night. Pods often work together to round up as much food as possible.

We've found some food! It's a whole bundle of tasty fish. I heard them from far away – so many fish make a lot of noise. I soon tracked them down using my ultrasound.

A tight ball of fish is called a bait ball.

We all work together to catch fish. A few of the others are circling the shoal. The fish are trying to swim away, but they all end up in a tight ball in the middle of our pod.

IN THE KNOW

Some bottlenose dolphins hold a sponge in their mouth while they look for food on the seabed. The sponge stops them scratching their beaks.

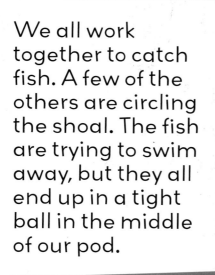

A few of us have found another meal. We've forced some of the fish onto the shore. They just flop around on the mud, making an easy meal.

Dolphins can leap onto sandy banks to snap up the stranded fish.

19

Snapping up food

Dolphins are not fussy eaters. They eat just about anything they can catch! Dolphins make it look easy, but it takes a lot of skill and practice to catch a meal under the sea.

We take it in turns to swim through the ball of fish. It's my turn now and they are getting away! I'll send out a blast of sound. That should slow them down.

Fast-swimming fish are stunned with a wave of sound to make them easier to catch.

FAVOURITE FOOD

Shellfish

Lobster

Squid

Fish

I grab slippery fish in my teeth. They struggle a lot but won't get away. A quick bite kills them. Then I swallow them whole in one gulp!

The dolphin's curved teeth hook into prey.

Meeting humans

When dolphins are close to the coast, they may meet humans. Some divers like to swim with dolphins and play with them, too.

I don't mind being touched by humans. This one is being very gentle with me.

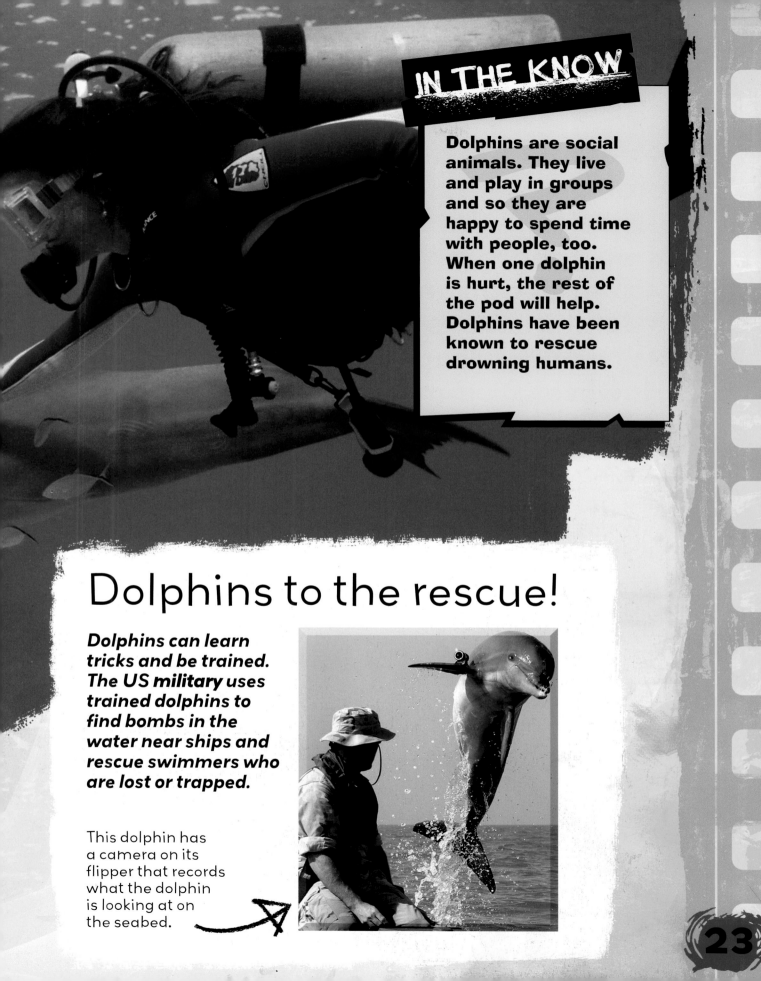

Dolphins are social animals. They live and play in groups and so they are happy to spend time with people, too. When one dolphin is hurt, the rest of the pod will help. Dolphins have been known to rescue drowning humans.

Dolphins to the rescue!

Dolphins can learn tricks and be trained. The US military uses trained dolphins to find bombs in the water near ships and rescue swimmers who are lost or trapped.

This dolphin has a camera on its flipper that records what the dolphin is looking at on the seabed.

23

Taking a rest

A dolphin has a very large brain. It uses it to make sense of all the sounds that it hears in the water. Like all animals, a dolphin needs to rest its brain by sleeping. However, it cannot sleep too deeply or it will stop swimming and drown!

I'm tired. It is time to head to a quiet patch of sea and have a sleep. I'm only ever half asleep, though. I still swim to the surface to breathe.

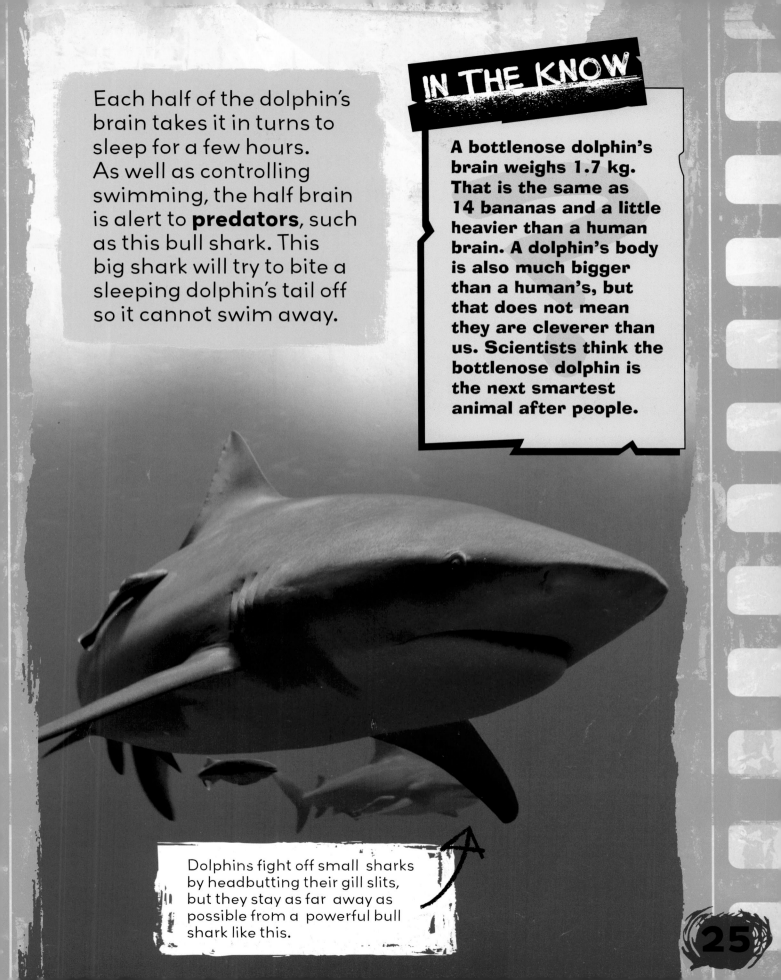

Each half of the dolphin's brain takes it in turns to sleep for a few hours. As well as controlling swimming, the half brain is alert to **predators**, such as this bull shark. This big shark will try to bite a sleeping dolphin's tail off so it cannot swim away.

IN THE KNOW

A bottlenose dolphin's brain weighs 1.7 kg. That is the same as 14 bananas and a little heavier than a human brain. A dolphin's body is also much bigger than a human's, but that does not mean they are cleverer than us. Scientists think the bottlenose dolphin is the next smartest animal after people.

Dolphins fight off small sharks by headbutting their gill slits, but they stay as far away as possible from a powerful bull shark like this.

Meeting a mate

When a female dolphin is ready to breed, she mates with several of the males in the pod. If she meets a new pod she may choose to live and mate with some new companions.

IN THE KNOW

Female bottlenose dolphins are ready to breed once they are almost fully grown. It can take anywhere between seven and 12 years to reach the right size. A female dolphin could have as many as ten calves in her life.

I have found a superpod. It has been a long time since I've seen so many dolphins. The males are not being so rough with me this time. They are all blowing bubbles to get noticed.

I like this male best, because he chases the others away. We swim off together. We play with each other and bump our heads together to show we are ready to mate.

WOW!

It takes 12 months for a dolphin calf to develop inside its mother. Human babies are born after about 9 months.

Saving dolphins

The bottlenose dolphin is one of the most common types of dolphin in the world. But many other types of dolphin are **endangered**. If people do not help them, some dolphins could become **extinct**.

Dolphins look for large shoals of fish, and so do fishing boats. Sometimes dolphins get caught in fishing nets. They can't reach the surface to breathe and so they drown. Fishing with smaller nets and lines is safer for dolphins.

Many fishing boats use huge nets to catch fish. This dolphin was lucky not to get caught.

When dolphins or whales get stranded, they need to be helped back into the water or they will die.

Ship engines, jet skis and even oil rigs make a lot of noise underwater. This can confuse dolphins. It could be one reason why dolphins sometimes get stranded on beaches.

太地よ、恥を知れ！
SHAME ON TAIJI

A few countries, such as Japan, still allow dolphin hunts. These people are protesting about it, saying that governments should ban the hunts.

QUIZ

1) What does a dolphin use its lower jaw for?

2) Without a nose, what do dolphins use for smelling?

3) Dolphins ride bow waves of a ship to: a) keep cool; b) save energy; c) listen to what people are saying?

4) How do dolphins stun fish?

5) What is a bait ball?

6) The name of a group of dolphins is a bop. True or false?

7) Why do dolphins die in fishing nets?

Answers:
1) A dolphin uses its lower jaw for hearing sounds.
2) Dolphins use their tongues for smelling.
3) b – to save energy.
4) Dolphins stun fish with a loud noise.
5) A bait ball is a shoal of fish trapped by dolphins.
6) False, it is a pod.
7) They cannot breathe and so they drown.

GLOSSARY

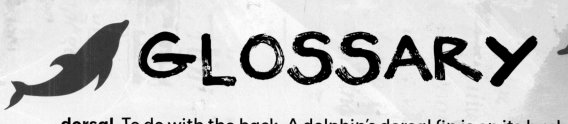

dorsal To do with the back. A dolphin's dorsal fin is on its back.

echolocation Bouncing sounds off objects to make echoes that tell an animal what is around it.

endangered When something is in danger.

evolve When a kind of animal gradually develops into something different.

extinct When all of one type of animal, or species, dies out forever.

female An animal that lays eggs or gives birth to young. The opposite type is a male, which cannot produce eggs or babies.

flukes The fins on a dolphin's tail that point sideways.

male An animal that does not lay eggs or give birth to young, but must mate with a female before she can be a mother.

mammal An animal that feeds its babies on milk and has at least a few hairs (dolphins have a few in their blowhole).

military Organizations that fight wars using soldiers, ships or aircraft.

pod A group of dolphins or whales.

predator An animal that hunts for other animals and then kills them for food. Dolphins are predators.

prey An animal that is hunted or killed by another for food.

taste bud A sensor on the tongue that picks up the taste of food.

Index